Jorge Benson

Gays in confession...

who am I to judge?

Buenos Aires

2014

What does a priest do, if a gay comes for confession?

Let us suppose that I am a priest, hearing confessions, and suddenly a person asks me if he can keep a Christian life, receiving the sacraments, without renouncing to a homosexual relationship.

Do we say: who am I to judge you?

I don't think it's enough.

It won't be enough for that person, who will ask for our opinion.

We'll have to respond.

And for that, we'll have to put the issue in the framework of the principles regarding sexuality.

And, then, we'll try to elucidate our pastoral approach to respond and be helpful to any homosexual person in their various situations: single, married, religious...

Index

I

The problem

We understand homosexuality as a predominant sexual orientation towards persons of the same sex. Or, in the words of an expert, the person who has a persistent erotic attraction to individuals of his or her own gender is homosexual.[1]

There are causes and degrees in homosexuality. And there are degrees in the freedom of the individual to overcome it, if he or she wishes to do so -- and thus in the moral responsibility.

There are those slightly inclined, and there are those strongly compulsive. There are those who have had homosexual experiences and do not really have a permanent inclination; there are those who have it and want to get rid of it; and there are, on the contrary, those making a flag of their homosexuality, and waving it in parades.

Therefore, if it is a question of judging, we'll have to consider, first of all, the possible causes and origin of the tendency, and the distinction between homosexuality as inclination and homosexuality as activity.

---

[1] Cfr. HARVEY, J., OSFS, *Chastity and the Homosexual*, en The Priest, July-Aug. 1977 (NY), p. 13.

II

The origin of the tendency

The origin of homosexuality is a matter of ongoing research. There are many theories that seek to explain this difficult problem, while continuing scientific research. For some, it comes from genetic elements, such as hereditary factors or poorly balanced hormones.[2] According to this homosexuality would be pre-moral.

Others (with dubious foundation and not very convincingly) pretend it to be a congenital brain problem, as there would be a sexual difference in certain fibers of the brain, which would determine the existence of three possibilities instead of two. Accordingly, homosexuality would be just normal.

It is generally (though not unanimously) accepted the idea that it comes from Psychogenic factors. And it is common opinion that homosexual orientation is not acquired in adulthood, but responds to situations of childhood or adolescence. In the absence of definitive conclusions, we prefer to talk, rather than of *causes*, in the strict sense, of *factors* that contribute to the genesis and development of homosexuality in a person.

Although it is difficult to find the exact cause in each case, the most frequent is that the inclination arises in childhood or adolescence by deficiencies in the family (a possessive mother, a negligent parent, a certain insecurity and fear of the opposite sex, etc.).

In this context of psychological -rather than physical- factors developed in childhood, recent studies point to the influence of the father, more than of the mother, in the development of homosexuality in males, and of the mother in the homosexuality in women. Let's not forget that the model of male and woman received at home is fundamental in the psychological affirmation of each person.

---

[2] BUCKLEY, M.J., *Summary of Research on heredity and hormonal factors..*, cit. by NCCB, *Principles to Guide Confessors In Questions of Homosexuality*, NCCB, Washington, 1973, p. 5.

Gay boys usually have a possessive mother and a negligent father. And they miss the identification with the father for their psycho-sexual affirmation.

Gay girls could have a mother who minimized their femaleness, instead of asserting them in it, and a father who leaves his wife to dominate on the entire family. Female model is then that kind of male-mother. Having a weak parent always contributes to it.

Homosexuality in girls may respond to the negative image of the father, and consequent contempt for the male image in general (e.g., if he is a drunkard, or weak, or if, to the contrary, beats the mother, etc.).

An important factor is the inability of a boy to form normal relationships with peers. A sickly boy, or over-protected, or who is denied to play with others for any reason (e.g. because *mom wanted a girl...* and just did not renounce to it). The boy sees his fellow entangled in games sometimes tough but always friendly, and feels left aside. It gets even worse when the others are cruel, and not very cooperative.

And then he shows up, the one that warmly opens his arms for him and offers him a relationship of psychological and physical protection. Our boy won't want to miss it, but rather to affirm it and to feed; although not always in a male fashion (his psychology is becoming female).

Another possible factor is emotional retardation. A boy or youngster can grow physically but may be -as some will claim- set in an emotional stage of narcissistic attraction. He loves himself, he grows that love, and becomes somehow determined (unconsciously) to love just what looks like himself. If he has the misfortune of falling into a homosexual experience, for the seduction of someone, or out of curiosity, etc., he can get oriented to keep looking in that way for that which he found pleasant.

Other factors include a certain fear of the opposite sex, some unhappy experience; the lack of opportunities for healthy contacts with youngsters of opposite sex; the lack of a normal family life (boarding);[3] an anti-sexual Puritanism as to look at girls as untouchables, and which can create the idea that there is not nothing wrong in relations with the same sex. There have been cases of homosexuality dues to promiscuity at home, even with the parents.

---

[3] Dr. Bieber says that, out of more than a hundred cases, he couldn't find in any of them a normal parental-son relationship, even if he tried to extend the concept of normal beyond the imaginable (cfr. NCCR, *ibidem*, 7).

We could add factors that contribute to an excessive shyness, such as stuttering, very pronounced acne, and everything that can induce to seek companionship and affection exclusively with the own sex, not only in adolescence, as it is normal, but entering the juvenile age, with risk of homosexual seduction.

As we see, we cannot speak of decisive factors in the history of any homosexual. Probably anyone of them is given isolated or exclusive.

III

Freedom of control?

If a gay wants to overcome the inclination, would he or she be free to do it?

To study their freedom of control of the inclination, we must begin by acknowledging different degrees of that tendency.

Among those who have a regular attraction, there are those who have so much control over its tendency as any heterosexual on his own.

At the other end, there are some openly compulsive, much like an alcoholic or a drug addict. As for the compulsive, it is known that they have a sort of fascination for an object, or a kind of obedience to an insurmountable impulse. From an initial weakness to resist it, they engender the conviction that this orientation is irresistible (a conscience illness, like scruple or laxity).

The psychological nature of this compulsive homosexuality can be known in the miserable and even dangerous circumstances in which many times it is unhindered (in other words, no normal person would be given to certain pleasures in public, uncomfortable and dirty places, as many homosexuals do).

Nevertheless, even the compulsive deserves and can receive an effective aid, to help them not to assent to their inclinations, and to get rid of them with appropriate therapy.[4] That compulsion does not imply a stronger sexual strength that in straight individuals. Rather -in the psychological jargon- an inability to adapt to internal tensions that threaten the balance of the personality. Heterosexuals may also have compulsions (masturbation, alcohol, drugs, etc.), that appear to be incorrigible.

---

[4] It is important to help people to assume and confront their psychological problems with the same open and natural attitude with which they attack physical diseases.

IV

So, can we judge?

Our gay penitent is still waiting, while we continue our analysis.

We mentioned above the possible causes of the tendency, and the distinction between homosexuality as *inclination* and homosexuality as a consented *activity*.

Some authors distinguish three levels, and that criteria may be useful: namely

- the potential orientation,
- the orientation as conscious attraction,
- and the activity.

a. The tendency can be found potentially in any person carrying the consequences of the original sin. That orientation can be controlled, with effort and the divine grace. Saint Augustin, inviting us to humility and caution, says that there is no sin committed by one person that another one cannot commit. *Therefore, whoever thinks he is standing secure should take care not to fall* (I Cor, 10, 12).

b. A conscious attraction towards people of the same sex is something more serious, and that is what we properly call homosexuality. It is the result of special circumstances, as we know, from parental indiscretions to a personal and adult decision to procure new sensations. In principle, this attraction is not itself a sin, that is to the extent that it doesn't include deliberate will (a habit already retracted, or a pathological condition requiring or under treatment), and might even be a chance to supernatural merit in the ascetic struggle.

c. Open and active homosexuality is the consent to the inclination. This is definitely contrary to the constant moral teaching of the Church.

Let's start by focusing on homosexuality as conscious attraction and habitual activity.

And here we are to distinguish between objective morality (or in-morality) of homosexuality, and the degrees of subjective responsibility of homosexuals.

1. The **objective** morality of sexuality can be founded on the teachings of the Church about marriage: according to this, genital expression between male and female takes place only within the framework of marriage. Objectively, the sexual relationship has a double intention: is a *procreative act of union*. None of these two purposes can be excluded, even if for different reasons the generative goal is not achieved. Sex is the expression of a fruitful love. That sexual expression should take place only within the framework of marriage, to the point that we could call the sexual act, *marriage act*, manifestation of the love between the spouses and ordained in itself to procreation, its natural purpose.

Homosexual activity, sexual intercourse between persons of the same sex, by its very nature excludes any possibility of procreation. Objectively it is a disorder, as it contradicts the natural inclination. Therefore it is a disorderly use of the sexual faculty, contrary to procreation and also to the expression of mutual love between husband and wife. It is not fruitful love. It is an act contrary to nature, and therefore contrary to the will of its Author.

The purpose of the sexual act, -act which engages the whole person, and the fulfillment of the human personality-, requires that the sexual act be performed within the framework of family life. Because procreation must be followed by the education of the child, engendered as a result of that union of love. The child is the incarnation of that love sealed with a definitive word, which expresses the commitment of the will.

All this is contrary to homosexual activity. Homosexual activity it's a deviation from the normal attraction -between male and female- which leads to the founding of a family. Homosexuals cannot, neither love each other with that fruitful love, nor complement each other as the male and female, made different and complementary. It is not surprising, therefore, that unions between homosexuals are not long-lasting.

We can say that it is a constant teaching. From the book of Genesis it is affirmed in the Scriptures the natural doctrine on marriage between man and woman: a union which St. Paul compares to that of Christ and the Church.

There are six references to homosexuality in the Scripture, five of men (Lev 18, 22; 20, 13;) Rom 1: 27; I Cor 6: 9-10; I Tm 1, 9-10) and one of women (cf. Rom 1: 26-27). The clearest is Romans 1: 26-27: *Therefore, God handed them over to degrading passions. Their females exchanged natural relations for unnatural, and the males likewise gave up natural relations with females and burned with lust for one another. Males did shameful things with males and thus received in their own persons the due penalty for their perversity.*

Whenever Paul mentions homosexuality, he vigorously condemns this attack on God's Plan. The immorality of homosexual activity is especially manifest in the context in which the Apostle writes. As pagans reject the worship of the true God, He lets them tumble in their vices in all forms, including unnatural practices, -very common in some towns (e.g. Corinth, to the point of being mentioned as *Greek love*)-. God punishes idolatry by depriving them of his grace, and without it the decline becomes inexorable.

Based on the Sripture, the Magisterium condemns it, especially in the Declaration on sexual ethics, of the Sacred Congregation for the doctrine of the faith, of November 7, 1975, approved by Paul VI[5], and more specifically in the Letter on pastoral care to homosexuals, October 1986. In July 1992, it develops the principles, in the Considerations addressed to the US bishops, on the occasion of certain legislative projects.

2. From the **subjective** point of view, a moral judgment of homosexual acts needs to consider the origin of the orientation, and how the person acts in accordance with or against it.

Normally the male or the female person does not want to become homosexual. Rather the person realizes, at one point of his or her life, that has such an inclination. And that leads to a certain trauma.

---

[5] There are different positions amongst the Protestants, as they lack of one magisterial criteria (cfr. the article in New York Times, 17-8-92).

The earlier the trend is found, the better it permits to face a professional treatment to reorient sexual desires and normalize the psychology. And -so far- it may be not yet a moral problem.

But maybe also possible that the person is or feels too old for that, or that the treatment is nor affordable, and gives up its possible solution -here the moral responsibility varies-.

A deeper understanding of the moral teaching of the Church, and of the possible causes of the homosexuality of that particular case, can help the candidate to better understand his or her situation and to act with greater freedom, decision and efficiency, towards personal fulfillment.

And the priest who wants to be helpful will be so if he analyses the various situations in which a gay person can find him or herself.

Then let's look at some elements that will help the pastoral work with gays.

But, before, let us hear an important contribution of the Holy See for our pastoral work:

"At the present time there are those who, basing themselves on observations in the psychological order, have begun to judge indulgently, and even to excuse completely, homosexual relations between certain people. This they do in opposition to the constant teaching of the Magisterium and to the moral sense of the Christian people. "A distinction is drawn, and it seems with some reason, between homosexuals whose tendency comes from a false education, from a lack of normal sexual development, from habit, from bad example, or from other similar causes, and is transitory or at least not incurable; and homosexuals who are definitively such because of some kind of innate instinct or a pathological constitution judged to be incurable.

"In regard to this second category of subjects, some people conclude that their tendency is so natural that it justifies in their case homosexual relations within a sincere communion of life and love analogous to marriage, in so far as such homosexuals feel incapable of enduring a solitary life.

"In the pastoral field, these homosexuals must certainly be treated with understanding and sustained in the hope of overcoming their personal difficulties and their inability to fit into society. Their culpability will be judged with prudence. But no pastoral method can be employed which would give moral justification to these acts on the grounds that they would be consonant with the condition of such people. For according to the objective moral order, homosexual relations are acts which lack an essential and indispensable finality. In Sacred Scripture they are condemned as a serious depravity and even presented as the sad consequence of rejecting God. (Rom. 1:24-27; cf. also 1 Cor. 6:10, 1 Tim. 1:10). This judgment of Scripture does not of course permit us to conclude that all those who suffer from this anomaly are personally responsible for it, but it does attest to the fact that homosexual acts are intrinsically disordered and can in no case be approved."[6]

---

[6] CONGREGATION FOR THE DOCTRINE OF THE FAITH, *Declaration on Certain Questions Concerning Sexual Ethics*, 29-XII-1975.

V

What do we do? The pastoral attitude

For those who have a habitual inclination, the moral principle states that every homosexual has to control their tendency by all the available means, in particular psychological resources and spiritual direction.

The Confessor should avoid both the hardness and the permissiveness. He must acknowledge that it is difficult for homosexual people to remain chaste in their environment, and that it is easy to relapse for various reasons: loneliness, compulsivity, the pressure of friends, etc.

But he should also know that homosexual is in general responsible for his activity, in either way. The worst thing that a gay person can hear is that he or she is exempt from liability.

This does not mean that gays are always able to easily get rid of temptation. Freedom is often limited and weak. But they must not be easily excused for their past. Their responsibility lies in the search for a greater strength of will, based on clear concepts and renewed motivation, and helped by a plan of ascetic life.

It is foreseeable that, despite the good resolutions that may arouse in the homosexual person, there will possibly be a relapse, due to long habits. But this should not be a reason for permanent excuse.

The pastoral care of homosexuals can diversify according to different situations. We should make a distinction, therefore, between occasional and permanent, men and women, married and religious.

Occasional gays

A guy confesses acts with another guy. It may be a momentary experience, due to curiosity, violence, etc. We have acknowledged the case of adolescents who, by the particular circumstances in which they live (for example in boarding schools), and the consequences of the original sin, have felt a special and casual attraction to someone of the same sex, which could have also led them to a fall, passed and forgotten. Pastorally, insofar as it has not engendered a habit, they should not be considered as homosexuals, nor led to a trauma that could make them doubt about their virility - or femininity - and the possibility of a normal life, either in family or Religion.

What is to be found out here is if the guy has, in fact, a homosexual inclination. In that case he needs encouragement them to seek help and a professional treatment, to then return to the Confessor for spiritual direction. The younger the guy, the more likely he is to be able to reorient his sexual tendencies and develop a total cure. He also needs reassurance to establish normal and stable relationships with other guys of both sexes, and all the help that is usually offered to those who have not that problem.

If it's the case of a young man with apparent homosexual inclination, we must remember that it is better to prevent than cure. The effort, which must be very generous, must tend to persuade the candidate of the urgent need to avoid occasions: groups of homosexuals, places frequented by them, or places of certain promiscuity, as showers or public changing rooms, conversations with strangers in public places, as readings and performances, related to the cultivation of the body, write intimate letters, etc. I.e., the care for the chastity of heterosexual persons, in their dealings with persons of the other sex, should apply.

Something analogous should be said about adults who have had a fall of this kind, perhaps due to the influence of alcohol or drugs.

What about prisoners, sailors, and people in similar situations? In prisons, for example, often happens that someone is given to homosexual acts for fear. Nonetheless, they are not entirely guiltless, although the responsibility is proportionally reduced because of the violence. Once back to liberty and normal social life this problem usually disappears.

Permanent homosexuals

In dealing with *permanent* gays, the Confessor can find two different cases: those coming for help, and those who come to discuss and be justified.

The ones who come to confession willing to be justified can pretend that the only human relationships, in which they find their fulfillment, are those of a homosexual type. They may need time to talk and calm down, but we will have to propose to discuss the case out of the confessional, as the only way to respond to their questions and needs.

The answer, for this as for all, is the possibility and need to live chastely. It is possible, and is crucial, and so we'll have to suggest a life plan that includes prayer and meditation, spiritual reading, the frequent reception of the sacraments, and some kind of regular commitment to charities. We must insist on spiritual direction and in the search of stable relationships. There is nothing like a stable friendship with someone, but this is one of the major difficulties in the life of a gay person.

The other case is the one who comes to seek help and wants to get out of his usual milieu. He doesn't need so much to be convinced of the immorality of his disorder, but a new motivation to get out of it. It is the case of someone who has had an experience of human affection and support, from others who are in the same situation, and is seeking help to get out of it to live something still better. This is one of the great challenges for every priest who hears confessions.

The basic reference is that he has to return to a heterosexual lifestyle. But, more specifically, he needs to be encouraged to find and form stable friendships. More than anyone, he needs a normal and deep human relationship.

Should we require, from him, to drastically cut off any friendship with another homosexual? Not always. Moreover, given that emotional need, it does not seem prudent, at first, forcing him to total solitude. It should be demanded not to coexist with other (it would be a next occasion of sin), and strongly advised to assert himself in good resolutions, with planning and spiritual direction.

This is, obviously, debatable and prudential. But it should not be assumed that every gay person needs absolutely to express genitally his or her relationship with another person. Let us remember that in homosexuality, especially among women, there is an affective dimension prior to a genital one. They need to support themselves in the affective dimension, in order to reorient the sexual drive.

A homosexual can lead a good spiritual direction and have progressed under it, and suddenly have a relapse with the person with which maintains a stable friendly relationship. In principle absolution shouldn't be denied it, with a warning to take every precaution not to fall again. If it becomes clear that it will happen again, in that relationship of friendship that was apparently a help to grow as a person, it must be definitely cut off.

Psychiatric treatment may be useful. But it cannot be imposed, as there can be psychological impediments (prejudice against this kind of professionals), economic difficulties, etc.

What happens if there are no perspectives of cure, of sexual reorientation?

This possibility must be accepted, and the pastoral help and spiritual accompaniment must go on.

The married gay

Here will raise issues of marriage validity.

In principle, every case deserves particular consideration. For example, the incontinent sailor, or the one in prison, who fall into acts of this nature (with no homosexual inclination), could be more about masturbation than about homosexual acts.

But there are some that are not ready for the ascetic struggle and sacrifice, and are unable to cope with a normal married life. Marriage in these circumstances would be null.

As consented inclination and usual activity, prior to the celebration of the marriage, it is canonically considered a ground for nullity,[7] as an impediment to the matrimonial duties. And this not only in a physical sense (could perform the *marriage act*) but affective, as support of the wife or husband and educator of their children.

The occasional homosexual activity, after the celebration of the marriage, could also be reason for invalidity if it demonstrates previous psychic disorders.

The first thing the Confessor must find out is if the penitent is homosexual, bisexual, or basically straight with occasional falls of homosexual type.

If it's the case of a habitual old-timer homosexual, unable to fulfill the duties of marriage, both affectively and sexually, their marriage would be invalid, since it could not comply with the conditions of the contract signed on the basis of that assumption. The canonical aspects should be referred to the Diocesan tribunal, alleged that the penitent agrees to transfer the matter from confession to the external jurisdiction.

But, if the person expresses ability to be husband or wife, despite some occasional falls, and wants to go on with their marriage, the Confessor should be supportive in that sense. To do this, he must ensure that the person wants to continue a serious spiritual direction and make use of the aforementioned resources.

---

[7] Cfr. CIC, c 1095.3:

It is possible that, in some cases, the gay part tells the other, hoping to have effective support to cope and eventually solve the problem, and so to save their marriage. That implies prudence against the occasions, a serious professional therapy and the help of supernatural means. This is, of course, a prudential question. Such a communications seems more advisable in the case of compulsive homosexuals, since in those cases the secrecy tends to increase tension and compulsion.

Lesbians

Homosexual women differ from men in the depth of his attachment to their partners, and in the duration or relative permanence of their relations. It is more common to find lesbian homosexual than men living a kind of permanent and faithful union. Relations between homosexual women are less physical than those between men, to the point that sometimes the physical action is scarce.

Women are also more receptive of advice than men, as well as easier to admit this homosexual tone in their relationships. But they will cling more strongly to them than men, especially - and always in that emotional level - by fear of the vacuum in which to cut them off would leave them.

They do not have the same need for physical expression of male. In many cases they could maintain the intimate bonding with the other part without any sexual expression, so it would be easier for them to avoid them –in order not to commit a sin-, compensating physical abstention with higher satisfaction on the affective level.

Faced with the moral need to cease such activities, they do not try to justify themselves, as men tend to do.[8] If she values the life of grace, she won't have difficulty in sublimating her sexuality, or at least try, putting the means to achieve it.

Another difference is that women have normally more pressure from the milieu than men, toward marriage. This has its disadvantages, because they

---

[8] I had a case of a young gay who for two hours displayed every possible reason for not giving up his chosen lifestyle. Needless to say that, in this conversation at a rational level, neither of us convinced the other. Or perhaps it is better to say that my reasons were not enough to move to a will that had already decided otherwise.

sometimes marry despite their inclinations, and the very probable invalidity is more difficult to prove that male homosexuality. As for the rest, it is pertinent here what has been said with regard to homosexual males.

The consacrated

We are going to refer now, separately, to religious, seminarians and priests, as to three different situations. Although, understandably, all three are closely related around the celibacy and the desire to fully live the virtue of chastity.

Religious

There is a specific reference in an official Document, which states that *those who do not seem suitable to overcome their homosexual tendencies, (...) must be dismissed from the religious life.*[9]

Let us highlight the expression: those who do not seem suitable to overcome the tendency...

These should not only be dismissed, but they should not have even entered, in the first place.[10] Their inclination is going to put them in occasion of sin. And their difficulties to interact in a normal friendship with members of the community will result in a life of permanent suffering.

Going a little deeper, there is a big difference between the way of approaching the vow of chastity in a religious heterosexual and one gay. Jesus speaks of renouncing sex and marriage for the Kingdom (cf. Mt 19, 12.29). It's not only resigning sexual enjoyment, but also the life of marriage to which one feels inclined, to intimacy with another person, with all that this means, in order to be free and focused on the service of God in the Church (cf. I Cor 7, 32-35).

Gay persons, entering religious life, could wish - in their psychology – to have a certain intimacy with someone to whom they feel inclined (and with whom they will live). Moreover, they could claim to fulfill, -as some would have it- their intimacy with the Lord through the intimacy with their

---

[9] Cfr. *Directives for the Formation in Religious Institutes,* Sacred Congregation for Institutes of Consecrated Life and Societies of Apostolic Life (13-11-90). Statistics claim that 80% of candidates for religious life in USA have homosexual tendencies. Religious meetings often discuss the topic, not always in line with the approach of the Holy See.

[10] SCANLON, R., *Homosexuals and the celibate*, Ufe, HPR, Oct. 1991 (NY), 22ss.

religious brethren, as it happens in marriage. [11]The stability of their religious life will thus depend on the stability of their relationship with *Brother X* or *Sister Y*. Just let us imagine the problems of the community when jealousies and tensions emerge.

At this point we could ask ourselves: it is not possible that two gays engage in a chaste relationship of friendship?

It would seem possible, as it is possible between straight male and female (e.g.: Saint Francis and Saint Claire). There are those who say that it could be beneficial, insofar as it is chaste, and not selfish or exclusive.[12] But among religious, it doesn't seem neither prudent nor motivating perfect chastity, taking into account the coexistence in common residence with the one who tends to get intimate.

Saint Francis wouldn't have lived in the same house with Saint Claire, in the same way as he didn't allow his brothers to enter in the convents of the Sisters but under severe constraints.

Here the principle is, obviously, that all who wish to live a Christian life must try to avoid near and unnecessary occasion of sin. Specifically, the religious, who is feeling and hiding a homosexual orientation, and lives in community, is in near occasion of sin, The most elementary prudence advises here the equivalent recommended separation between religious male and female

In religious life, as in seminaries, there is not only the problem of the lack of vocations, but of *false* vocations.

The best way to avoid both is clearly teach the essence and excellence of the vocation to the consecrated life. That will prevent from knocking at the door those candidates with more emotional than spiritual motivations.

Personally I believe that a youngster who does not like girls cannot have vocation. Because, to begin with, there would not be the renunciation of something good and dear for something better. (cf. Mt 19, 29; Le 18, 29). Nobody can offer in sacrifice what he does not have. In his case, it could not give that resignation to the genital expression of the gift of self in love to a person of opposite sex, for that supreme form of that self-giving that

---

[11] Ibidem, p. 24.

[12] Cfr. ibidem, pp. 24-25.

constitutes the very meaning of human sexuality, in the words of St. John Paul II.[13]

With gays, as with the sexually impotent, it would not be the case of becoming *eunuchs for the Kingdom of heaven...* (cf. Mt 19:12). They are already, somehow, for another cause.

Nobody is free to *renounce the conjugal love of another person of the same sex,* but everyone is so intended by nature (cf. I Cor 6, 9; Rom 1, 26).

In conclusion, what is to be done with the gay that wants to consecrate to God and live in chastity, as much as possible?

In principle it would seem possible, and that could be the best way to ensure eternal salvation -but avoiding the life in community-. Because community life would become, for him or her, a near occasion of sin. And also because his or her vow of continence wouldn't be an eschatological sign as celibacy, offered as a sacrifice for the Kingdom of heaven.[14]

Seminarians

Let us apply to seminarians, taking account of the differences, the same mentioned principles.

Here too we must clarify, usually with the help of a professional - psychologist - if we have a case of occasional homosexual sentiment or a true homosexual orientation.

The case of the adolescent seminarian who has an occasional drop should be examined particularly.

If it responds to a homosexual orientation, the seminarian should be advised to follow psychiatric treatment, because usually the person has other problems apart from the homosexual condition. This creates serious doubts about the permanence of the candidate in the Seminary, as in religious life.

---

[13] Cfr. *Familiaris Consortio,* 37.

[14] Cf. *Lumen Gentium* 44; *Perfectae Caritatis* 12.

In the case of a candidate who has had several falls of this kind, there must not be a hesitation to deny him absolution unless he leaves the Seminary, since the prospects of a healthy priestly life are scarce.

The fundamental criterion is to determine if the candidate is going to have so many difficulties in his priestly life to maintain chastity, that this will be a permanent source of unhappiness, tensions and eventually falls, scandals and deformation of the conscience in himself and others.

Also he who masturbates frequently with homosexual fantasies, for example, is demonstrating deep psychological problems.

In general, the doubts should be resolved in favor of the People of God, and in favor of the same candidate. And very much so, because his departure from the Seminary will most likely avoid a serious spiritual and emotional harm on himself, and later scandals in those who could be dealing with the problem and suffering its consequences in the future.

Abundant chronicles in recent times spare us from elaborating.[15]

Priests

The problem here is analogous: similar in terms of vocation to perfect chastity (so it is valid what was said above), and different as now we are talking about priests.

As we have said, there are different degrees of homosexuality. The priest with occasional falls must begin by examining the type of cases in which he has fallen.

They often respond to a combination of frustration and depression, need to escape, alcohol, and perhaps the frequent dealing with homosexual people.

He acts, in those cases, as any heterosexual priest may act under similar motivations, sinning *naturally* against chastity. This means that the homosexual priest can and must be led to understand that, in both cases, a ~~priest tends to fall when he loses~~ sight of the reasons that prompted him to

---

[15] A number of dioceses who are dealing with cases of homosexuality and pedophilia started the good practice, now well spread, of ensuring this aspects before receiving candidates or even priests from other countries.

engage for life to the priesthood and the Love of Christ. He needs help to revive the fervor and to reeducate himself in the ideal of perfect chastity.

The Priest deeply involved in homosexual activity, usually does not take it as a matter of his confessions, if he did not abandon the confession completely, convinced that it is not a sin or at least not something very serious. These priests need a complete spiritual rehabilitation, in which both the spiritual director and therapist are needed. Usually they want it, despite the verbal justifications that they can try. Their need conscience *recycling,* prayer and hope, so to overcome the problem.

Some countries have implemented institutes dedicated to the rehabilitation of priests and religious [16] -at least for those who want to leave the problem behind.

Because there are, also, like many lay people, those making of their homosexuality a cause to stand for.

---

[16] For example in New México, USA.

The activists

If there are gay pre-oriented by the circumstances, and there are active *in the closet*, there are also activists, those who argue in favor and promote their condition, claiming legal recognition in the name of non-discrimination.

Among Catholics, there are those seeking the right to receive the sacraments as any other member of the Church. They see homosexual activity as normal for them, and, in the same way that heterosexuals can establish relationships of fidelity and psychological-sexual complement, thus homosexuals have the right to do so and to complement each other.

It is true, say authors of the movement pro-Gay, that they may have to live in certain promiscuity, before formalizing a stable union. But ¿is it not what happens – they ask - with heterosexuals before marriage, with their passionate pre-nuptials encounters?

This way of life, they say, does not have to exclude them from the sacraments: as one tries to serve God and neighbor, sexual orientation is a matter of lesser importance and no consequence... Just look at the general way of living, and not to sexual level and its options.

To that, the Church responds with patience and firmness, showing the error of pretending that each one can vary their sexual expressions according to their sexual orientation and preference.

Conclusion

Gay persons need a patient and charitable pastoral dedication.

And we must provide them with a viable alternative, despite the difficulties that they face to live in chastity, in a plan that should include:

- prayer, sacraments, spiritual direction, ascetic;
- where possible, professional psychological treatment dedicated to its sexual reorientation.
- at least one stable relationship of friendship.
- some form of service to God and neighbor.

Many gay persons are already using and appreciating some help of this kind.

And many more are willing to decide and persevere in the effort towards a Christian way of living, both in the secular as in consecrated life.

BIBLIOGRAPHY

CATECHISM OF THE CATHOLIC CHURCH, III, 2, 2, a 6, 2357-9.

CONGREGATION FOR THE DOCTRINE OF THE FAITH, *Declaration on Certain Questions Concerning Sexual Ethics*, 29-XII-1975.

CONGREGATION FOR THE DOCTRINE OF THE FAITH, *Letter to the Bishops of the Catholic Church on the Pastoral Care of Homosexual Persons*, 1-X-1986.

CONGREGATION FOR THE DOCTRINE OF THE FAITH, *Some Considerations concerning the Catholic Response to Legislative Proposals on the Non-Discrimination of Homosexual Persons"*, 6-6-1992.

ST. JOHN PAUL II *Allocution (on the occasion of the approval of "marriage" of homosexuals by the European Parliament)*. 8-II-1994

U. S. NATIONAL CONFERENCE OF CATHOLIC BISHOPS, *Principles to Guide Confessors in Questions of Homosexuality* (1973);

U. S. NATIONAL CONFERENCE OF CATHOLIC BISHOPS, *To Live in Jesus Christ* (1976);

U. S. NATIONAL CONFERENCE OF CATHOLIC BISHOPS, *Called to Compassion and Responsibility* (1989);

U. S. NATIONAL CONFERENCE OF CATHOLIC BISHOPS, *Always Our Children* (1997).

PONTIFICAL COUNCIL FOR THE FAMILY, *Family, Marriage and "de facto" Unions,* July 26, 2000.

www.ingramcontent.com/pod-product-compliance
Lightning Source LLC
Chambersburg PA
CBHW070242290526
45789CB00004B/1728